Everything Changes

A *Spiritual Journey*

Stan Biderman

art by
Carolyn H. Manosevitz

To Darla ☆☆ *we heal together!*
Stan Biderman

Plain View Press
P.O. 33311
Austin, TX 78764

512-441-2452
sbpvp@eden.com

ISBN: 0-911051-87-2
Library of Congress: 96-069455
Copyright Stan Biderman, 1996.
Art copyright carolyn h. manosevitz.

Cover: Detail from "the survivor," caligraphy
by carolyn h. manosevitz, poem by
benhacohanim. Cover design by Matt Hovis.

Title Page Graphic: Detail, "the survivor," caligraphy by
carolyn h. manosevitz, poem by benhacohanim.

*This book is dedicated
to healing.*

Thanks

So many people have contributed to this book in knowing and unknowing ways. This book would not have been possible if it were not for all of you who shared yourselves with me in 12-step meetings and showed me a path to a personal Higher Power. I am eternally grateful for your courage, recovery, teaching and inspiration.

Likewise to my friends at Le Pavillon, now of North Carolina, thanks for sharing your love, your commitment to recovery, and for opening my eyes to the world of metaphysics.

To my longtime mastermind partners: Irene Watson, Mel Waxler, Jean Backus. You share in this visualization.

To Susan Bright and Margo LaGattuta, editors of Plain View Press, for accepting me as an equal, for treating my writing with respect, for sharing your experience and supporting my voice, for encouraging me along the way.

To Matt Hovis for your beautiful work with the cover art design.

To Carolyn Manosevitz for believing in me before I was able to believe in myself, and for continuing to believe in me. For your determination and vision.

To my sisters, Linda Hoffer and Ann Biderman for unwavering support. To my parents, Max and Helen Biderman, for their willingness and courage in sharing some incredibly difficult information.

To my wife, Linda, and my children, Andrea and Zach. Thanks for your love, support and guidance, listening, patience and tolerance as I have become a writer.

Contents

Epilogue   97

We have but two choices—
God or insanity.

i run as fast as i can
deep into the woods and i fall asleep on the ground...

9

Preceding Page: "the forest," 9 1/2" x 7," ink on paper, © carolyn h. manosevitz, 1996.

Interviews with Mailech and Chinka

War changes everything. Where there were rules before, war dictates even infinitesimal nuances of daily life, and daily life becomes a surreal mixture of tradition and hell.

In 1939, Germany begins bombardment of Lukow, Poland. Jews from other cities and towns are being rounded up and sent to Lukow, as the Germans are in the beginning stages of their plans for the Jews. Restrictions begin on where Jews can live. Prominent Jews are often rounded up and sent to prison.

What follows is a series of excepts from conversations between the author and his parents who are survivors of the Holocaust.

"family tree," © carolyn h. manosevitz, 1996.
On the right is the family tree of Chinka (Helen Prengler), the author's mother. On the left is the family tree of his father, Mailech (Max) Biderman. Each branch is a generation. Broken lines indicate those who are deceased.

13

Mailech hears two Orthodox Jews talking one day. The first orthodox man asks, *"Why did God let the Germans kill so many Jewish people?"* The second replies, *"Listen, you shouldn't ask any questions about God."*

The first replies, *"Why don't I have the right? When Moses took the Jewish people out of Egypt, they had no food, they had no water, and Moses asked God, 'Why did you take the Jewish people out to suffer in the wilderness?' If Moses could ask the question, I can ask the same question too."*

Mailech: *"We stay, but we are on the lookout. We don't have a choice. We are like rats that run from one place to another, knowing that people are following to kill us."*

"Everybody is hoping for time…We think 'maybe, maybe, maybe, maybe, maybe…' We stay in the same one or two barracks farthest away from the street. But they (the Nazis) find out. They come at 5 a.m. It is still dark. Everyone is still sleeping on the floor. I can hear them say 'Aufshtein!' or Wake Up! in their tough German voices. I know then that there is no chance to run away. We are surrounded."

"I say to myself, 'Let me go to the windows, to the door, to see if there is someplace, an opening, where we can run out, where we can run away.' I go to the windows where I see some Ukrainian soldiers and some SS people patrolling the building. I look in the back of the building. There is a large wooden door. The door is nailed to the building. Me and another six, seven or eight people say we are going to push the big door out and run, because what do we have to lose? What can we lose? We can hear the squeezing of the door opening, and we run out….We run into a field of farmland. We run out and it is dark, and it is raining just a little bit, and we can hear the machine guns. I don't know how many people get killed and how many don't, but I manage to run away."

"I'm sure my father and mother are happy that they have a place to sleep. Where I stay, I sleep in a closet. They put a few families in one room. I get sick there, typhus. Many people can't take it (the typhus) but I survive."

✡

Chinka: "When we come to the ghetto, Tatasha's (my Father's) sister is in one room with another sister and Israel (my father's brother), and they manage to give us one little room for over twenty people. The first night, I stay up all night, it is cold. I don't have anywhere to sleep; people, young kids are freezing outside.

I still feel strong about God, but I question what has happened to the little kids. I am taught that you always trust God and things turn out for a reason, but I don't see a reason for killing little babies that didn't do anything wrong....Even when we are hiding, we still observe the holidays."

April 1943: "We leave when they surround the ghetto and shoot my grandfather. The first thing in the morning, they surround the ghetto, we hear them all around the barbed wire. I am just over typhus. Mamasha (Chinka's mother) is running down to that place where we hide underneath the toilet. A few people come running, you can't let them in, you have to tell them to go away, everybody is fighting for his life. My grandfather and my uncle Isaac are running up towards the attic. I start running with them. In the middle of the steps, I change my mind and decide I am going down with my mother. When we go down, they are shooting and we hear people screaming as they drag them out. Around noontime, we hear them return with a chimney sweeper who knows my grandfather well from the brickyard. He comes searching the house. He doesn't find us, but he finds my grandfather and his son inside the attic of the house. It is a little wooden house. They take my grandfather down, and my uncle down. They (my grandfather and uncle) beg the Germans 'Please don't kill me' and we hear the screams and we hear the beggings and they shoot them, and they put them on wagons."

✡

Mailech: "*We have a hiding place underneath the wooden floor, but to me this is silly. The Nazis know, they have the experience, to find places where people are hiding. One day they surround the ghetto and they take me out, me and the other people. They take me to the railroad station and they put me into the cars.*

"*When I am close to the gas chambers, about fifteen miles away, the people in our train wagon discuss jumping. Many are unwilling to jump, because it is very risky, with the train going full speed. 'Besides,' they say, 'risky or not risky, if I jump, where would I go? There is no food, nothing to eat.' But me and another few boys break a hole through the door and manage to put our hands through and push back the door.*

"*I am the first one to jump from our wagon. A few people jump from other wagons. I jump out, and I can hear the machine guns. On every wagon, there are soldiers sitting with machine guns. They know that there will be some people jumping out. BRDRDRDRR you can hear the machine guns! I lie down with my face to the ground, like I am dead, and when I hear the last train wagon pass by, I raise my head. I see a woman, a young woman. I know her well. She is about two or three hundred feet from me. She jumped from another wagon. Blood all over, she is hurt very, very much. She is crying out for help. I can't help her. I know that German soldiers and their supporters, Polish people, will go by the railroad tracks to look for the Jewish people to catch them, take away whatever they have in their pockets, and turn them over to the Germans. I look out and I see some woods not far from here. I can't help the woman, and I know I am in danger, one-hundred percent. I run as fast as I can; I run, it is maybe a half a mile, or farther. I run as fast as I can, deep into the woods. I run deep into the woods and I fall asleep on the ground.*"

"I don't practice in the woods. We don't have Bibles; we don't have tefillin. Somedays we really didn't know whether it is Sunday, Monday, Tuesday, or Wednesday. My beliefs are changing some. I say I still believe in God, but I ask, 'How is this possible? Why did you let the Germans do the things they did?' I have questions."

"I fear the snow, because in the snow one can more easily be found. One day a friend is singing a Jewish tune. Another member of our group quickly pipes up, 'You had better be quiet. Don't sing the Hebrew song. We don't want God to know where we are.'"

Chinka: "Motkitskie is a kind man. He gives us a sense of hope. 'Be quiet,' he says, 'and you will live through the war.' Unfortunately, a less friendly Pole reports that we are hiding at Motkitskie's, and our exile begins again. We return to the brickyard and continue our hiding. At night, my brother Isaac runs down to the small pond and returns with a sip of water for all, the water is covered with bugs. In spite of that, the best champagne would not taste as good as a that sip of water does."

"I celebrate Passover with matzo baked in a small oven and with beet juice substituted for wine. In spite of a high fever, I fast on Yom Kippur, while we hear the Germans shooting outside. I don't think God has abandoned me, but I question. At times I am angry with God."

Mailech: "*After the war in Munich, I start a Jewish life again. It isn't a Jewish life like it was when I was very religious, but I start a Jewish life. I wear a hat all of the time....In Munich, there is a place on Isatoreplatz. There used to be a restaurant there. The people come every Saturday to pray. The Jewish Community Center has opened a kitchen for some people who don't have any money, to have lunch. It's a fact that we pray there every Saturday.*"

"*We go to this other city to find out whether we can buy something or sell something. There I meet this guy who used to be in our religious school, and he kept on until the war. He greets me so happily....He says, 'Oh, Mailech, I'm so glad to see you, to see that you lived through the war. I'm going to fix you something to eat with my wife. It's chazer (pork).' I bring out this story to tell the way people change....I did eat some pork in the woods. I didn't have a choice. But after the liberation, I wouldn't touch it, and he still does. OK? You got the whole story?*"

Chinka: "*We are still very orthodox. We never drive on Yom Kippur, never drive on Shabbas (the Sabbath)....I keep Kosher. There are rabbis, and shochtem (Kosher butchers)....It is not as orthodox as before the war. It is more worldly. This is a big city. We take on some customs....*

"*The trip to America takes two weeks. It is a terrible trip....The men and women are separated. It is not convenient at all. We have to climb a very tall ladder to get out on the deck. As soon as we move away from the coast of England, the water becomes very choppy. The water comes into the boat and covers us, and we become terribly seasick, every one of us.*"

18

✡

They reach port on September 21, 1949, and board a train for Dallas, Texas. Two days later, they celebrate a New Year and a new life on Rosh Hashana. And with their new home, they become not Chinka and Mailech, but Helen and Max.

✡

Max: *"It is hard for me to work on Saturday, but I know I have a wife and a child and I have to make a living. I do feel guilty. I don't work every Saturday, but sometimes when they ask me to work I have to work....I don't think about whether God will punish me. I don't want to think about it too much. I have some different thoughts. I am scared of the thoughts I am thinking....It is confusing."*

"But I know one thing. Many Jewish people are not religious. But before they die, if their memory is still good, and they know it's the last few minutes, they say, 'Shema Yisrael Adonai Eloheynu Adonai Echod,' the most basic of all Hebrew prayers. That will tell you something about people, even if they are not religious Jewish people. Before he dies, the Jew says, 'God of Israel, this is our only God.'"

✡

Helen: "It is hard for me. In the beginning it is hard. I don't feel good about it....I feel guilty, not like God is going to punish me, but I feel guilty....I still have Kosher chicken brought in from Dallas weekly....We do drive on Shabbas....We have Shabbas dinner at home every Friday. I always light the candles. Uncle Bloom comes and looks through the window, and he enjoys it because he came from a very orthodox family. His daddy was a Rabbi in Miedzyrzecz....They don't observe Shabbas that much, so it means a lot. So he comes and sneaks in and he enjoys it very much."

"We are not religious now....Things don't mean as much to me....I was more religious before....I just don't believe as strongly....Before I usually wouldn't have money or spend money on Saturday....Now I let my children buy ice cream on Saturday. I do things I wouldn't have done before....I believe (in Judaism) deep in my heart, but I feel like some changes need to be made...."

"The tradition, being a Jew, is more important to me than anything else. My belief in God is the most important. It doesn't matter if it's Orthodox, Conservative, but deep in me, the way I was brought up and the way I see the people dying and on their lips 'Shema Yisrael'....For those Jews who perish, I feel very strongly that I need to continue in the link of Judasim and tradition. It doesn't matter if it's that orthodox or whatever; it's mostly traditions and continuation of the traditions of generations previous....The culture is my life."

"I'm happy about the way it turned out. I just wish that some questions I have...that I could get answers....Like why it happened to the children who died for no reason at all. It's always on my mind....It is confusing. But I don't try to change it, because I'm not going to be able to, so I'm at peace with it....When I was growing up they said that the Messiah would come."

20

✡

Max: "I still believe in being Jewish. If there's a God, where is our God? There should be more…more God."

"If you ask me if I want my children to be like I was in the time when I enjoyed my life, I would say 'No.' The reason I would say no is that I believe you have to teach your children some kind of profession. If you study all of the time, and you don't have a profession, how can you support a wife? The Bible tells you that every parent should teach his child a profession, a shoemaker, a tailor, whatever it is, to be able to support a wife, support children. The way it was when I enjoyed my life is just study and study and study and study and study. My father told me at the time when I studied less that he would like for me to study more, and to be less involved in the poppy seed oil factory."

"Who do you think survived? The few people who survived had to be tough, tough people. A religious man, a very religious man, is not a tough person….How did I survive? It's not about learning fast. I have to say it was luck. The first time I ran away, the second time I ran away, when I jumped from the train, whatever I did…sure you have to be brave to do what I did. But I'm sure there were many more people, brave people, who just didn't make it."

Like seeds on the winds of the Diaspora, Max and Helen's children drift apart in the new world….

"the swing," 18" x 18," mixed media, © carolyn h. manosevitz, 1994.

The Survivor

The Survivor

Yit-gadal v'yit -kadash
>Piece by piece

Sh'mey raba
>ounce by ounce

Amen.
>life was taken from him.

B'alma di v'ra hirutey, v'yam-lih mal-hutey
>It didn't happen all at once

B'ha-ye-hon uv-yomey-hon uv-ha-yey d'hol beyt yisrael
>but day by day, death by death,

Ba-agala u-vizman kariv, v'imru: Amen
>the light left his eyes.

Y'hey sh'mey raba m'varah l'alam ul-almey alma-ya.
>*The souls of millions swirl in the hot wind.*

Yit-barah v'yish-tabah v'yit-pa-ar v'yit romam v'yit-na-sey
>It happened on the day he jumped from the cattle car

V'yit-hada v'yit-aleh v'yit-halal sh'mey d'kud-sha
>and on the day his parents were dragged
>into the street and shot.

B'rih hu, l'eyla min kol bir-hata v'shi-rata
>It happened when he ate pork as well as when he wept in
>hunger;

Tush-b'hata v'ne-hemata da-amiran b'alma v'imru amen
>bits of life taken, never to be wholly rekindled.

Y'hey sh'lama raba min sh'ma-ya
Though he lived, he died a thousand deaths

V'ha-yim aleynu v'al koy yisrael
which he passed on to his children

V'imru: Amen.
whose lights flickered erratically on their pedestals.

Oseh shalom bi-m'romav, hu ya-aseh shalom
His success was the success of a survivor

Aleynu v'al kol yisrael, v'imru: Amen.
who came to the feast of life without fork or knife.

Marsha's Lament

This piece was written after my father spoke to a group of middle-school children in Austin, Texas. Marsha Warenoff, a teacher at Kealing Middle School and my good friend, arranged the appearance.

Her eyes drowning in tears, she observes,
"Sadness is etched in his face."
The receding gray hairline,
deep, gentle brown eyes fill with visions
of the carnage
of his youth.
One furrow in his brow
the senseless death of a sister,
another, a brother,
a third deeply reminds of tortures
unknown by those
outside the inferno.

Lips frame the echo
of what once would have been a smile,
what is now a courageous attempt
to seize the moment;
jaws behind are pursed tight
by memories of
fifteen hundred days
wrought with degradation and death.

The old man speaks gently
of horror long ago—
embers of twinkles in his eyes
glow of his love, his compassion, his hope.
As she listens,
his words are inconceivable,
yet true.
She hears with
a woman's compassion

the depth of pain;
and she weeps the rivers
he cannot weep for himself.

His jowls sag.
Muscles worn thin by the weight
of the memories—
he fights to keep his chin up
but like his past it has
long fallen.
Gravity pulls everything down—
the gravity of his life is no exception.
Messages from his brain
pull from within;
memories join with Mother Nature
to tear down his face.

He began an ascetic;
ends a survivor.
An unteachable journey,
yet he has lived to tell the story.
The God of his youth works in mysterious ways.
The man has no explanation for Him now—
yet has some inward drive
(as a mother longs to tell the story
of her miscarried child)
to tell his story—
with hope for the future.

She looks one last time
before turning to leave—
her eyes well once more,
her heart aches with the grief
of places which she has the grace
never to have been.

She is afraid to go

and wants more,
wants an explanation,
the meaning
some meaning—
the only true meaning is
the tearing of her heart
as she studies
the sadness
that
is
etched
in
his
face.

The Valley of Thighs

Startled!
I am thrust into the world.
Shocked between thighs of conflict—
a thunderous vise of hatred crushes from the east
while the smothering grip of protectionism
suffocates from the west.

There's no air in here!

The forces of the crucible explode;
thrust from sultry, idyllic swampland
into bright lights,
shot from the womb
through pubic minefields,
spinning like an errant wheel—
Bump Thump Bump
bounding blindly down the path,
a wheel driven by conflict bound to crash;
the push and pull too great
until the inevitable topple-over.

I run back to protection
to the maternal thighfield,
as I cower for a safe shadow.
The sun is directly overhead
and there is nowhere to hide.
Exhausted in their own marathon
the thighs are like pistons
knocking me this way and that,
overworked pistons
locked in their own conflict,
a 100 years' war begun long before
I glimpsed first light.

The war is not over—

there is no finish line.
Even a marathon must have a finish line
but pistons beget other pistons,
industrial cylinders of perpetual torment.
I struggle to escape but am
blinded by the midthigh sun.
The thighs are a trap,
entrance to a vortex
which sucks life's marrow
from it's gravitational field.
Pistons run amuck
on an engine fueled by fear, by pain.

Slimed with the afterbirth of war,
my truth obscured
my vision clouded
I am taken cageless prisoner,
caged by maternal memories—
a lifetime of scrubbing and cleansing
wringing and scouring
scrubbing and cleansing
wringing and scouring
scrubbing and cleansing
scrubbing and cleansing
scrubbing and cleansing
and wiping soiled memories
passed from placenta through
thighs.

RAGE!

Delicate mask
sunken, hollow eyes
muted response
to a question barely heard.

Instantaneously
RAGE!
like an avalanche
in one cascading moment,
leaving no survivors.

Lulled into a sense of sanity
but the train has left the station;
wheels in my heart turn, build,
the power of the locomotive
spewing, hissing, screaming—
black cold ugliness
of acidic electricity surges
from temple through torso.

Shortness of breath
heaving of heart
boiling of blood
pupils shrinking
soldiers marching on
CLANG CLANG RAP RAP
ATTACK!!!
RAGE!

The swift, masked executioner leaves no survivors;
an efficient warrior
total in his destruction—
the hooves of Khan's soldiers arrogantly
trample their victims,

maiming, plundering, and raping
as rage gallops through their trust and innocence.

The Devil roars
the blood boils
the earth shreiks
the serpent coils
slashing striking then skulking,
feigning sorrow for a barb
plunged deeply into the
delicate spirit
of an unsuspecting victim.

Blinding hell's fire
explodes instantaneously!
Smoldering in the bowels
of a now confused tyrant;
cancerous embers
burn patiently of
illusive slights long forgotten,
as echoes of hooves die in the distance.

Running in shame
the Executioner
hears Abraham's bleating ram,
looks down at his blood-stained hands
aghast, afraid, and ashamed
at his deed.
The ram cries for Isaac and for Sarah.
For trust betrayed
by the incisive blade
of terror uncaged
by the grim reaper,
infectious carrier
of
RAGE!

The Cloak

When I was three
the gates slammed shut on my soul.

Nazi tormentors in high black leather boots
stomping the field of my innocence.

When I was five,
I played with rage
while others played with trains.

Fantasies of a new bicycle barely
interrupted my true fantasies.
I dreamt of being invisible,
of anonymity not based in hide and seek,
but in a much darker game.

I dreamt of machine guns and Germans.
I mowed them down
in gleeful play—
Rat tat tat
Gotcha!

This one's for my uncles!
This one's for my cousins!
And these for my grandparents,
you nasty sons of bitches!
They fell, I laughed.
It was play.

Frightfully, as I look into the
mounds of dead German bodies
I notice a white robe, or is it a cloak?
It looks out of place,
unseemingly pure in evil surroundings.

Momentarily, my confusion subsides
and I recognize it.
It is my childhood, taken long ago.
I left it in the field with the machine gun.

When I was three, the gates
slammed shut on my soul. . . .

I Am You

I am a Nazi.
You taught me how to be one
o' butcherous nation.

Your legacy bisects my life.

> I am your cruelty
>
> your numbness
>
> your will to destroy
>
> your unbending stubbornness
>
> your vicious punisher
>
> your relentless self-liar
>
> your sadistic gameplayer
>
> your arrogant justifier
>
> your killer of souls
>
> your legacy for generations.

O' sick nation,
you taught me well,
and now I am you.

You Might Not Think

You probably don't look at
that last sip of water
and think
it could've saved a life,

or put on that warm wool
and think about how comforting
it would've been
to starving bodies,
freezing in the rain.

You probably take for granted
that your first menstruation
would be held in the privacy,
dear privacy,
of a warm home.

That you can protect your family.

You probably don't look at
the last crumbs of bread
or grizzled bone
or grapefruit rinds
and see feasts that last three days.

You probably don't realize
that you could lose fifty pounds
and continue to live
on morsels of air.

You might think you would die
from typhus,
or rat bites,
or from living
day after day in darkness.

It might not occur to you,
as you sit in your warm bath,
that the warmth might have saved a life,
unable to hold on for those
few extra moments.

You might not imagine,
devise, create
scheme after scheme
of escape from imaginary captors.

You might not fantasize
about destroying thousands of people,
enjoying being invincible
and glowing in their pain.

You might not want to laugh
as they suffered at your cruelty
impervious to the reality
of your dream.

You might see that
atrocities breed hatred,
that once begun,
the cycle never stops.

You might feel superior
to your neighbors,
other races
or nations.

You probably don't look at
that last sip of water
and think
it could've saved a life. . . .

I do.

I Don't Get It

They say we must forgive you—
I don't get it.

How does one forgive
the executioner
who gloats with blood-stained hands?

How does one forgive the butcher
who kills for fun

the doctor who cuts deeply for pain

the welder who welds shut the door

the speaker who speaks only lies

the politician

the neighbor's turned face

the priest who long ago incited hatred

the engineer who drove the train

the impotent pissant Fuhrer

the hoards who followed him

the liars who now claim they didn't.

They say we must forgive you.
I know they are right—
I still don't get it.

Survivors of War

We are survivors of war.

I sit like a roasted carcass
small flies roosting in the hairs of my
forearms and legs
where the skin shows outside my
shorts and t-shirt.

The battle is over
and I am defeated;
I can't figure it out.
I've tried and
tried
and
Tried
and
TRIED!
GODDAMIT!
but trying changes nothing.

I work my muscles into chains of small locks,
fighting to unlock one, then the other,
only to have the gatekeeper hurriedly
lock them again.
Exhaustion rakes through
as I push and push forward
only to find that the world pushes back
with greater force.

I try my knees once again
but they recoil from true surrender.
I kneel in the illusion of prayer,

praying the best I know how.
It never seems enough.

I fight, I control, I attempt to surrender.
Using my password, I seek to gain entry
into serenity, into God,
only to find a sole dark tunnel in the midst of sunshine.

I learned to fight, learned to struggle
early in life.
It was our way.

The ways of lightness were foreign to my being
for when the doors clanged shut
the gatekeeper hid the keys
and left my people with keys to locks
thrown asunder.
We scurry to open the locks
finding only the mirror's trick
of door after door after endless door.

Our souls carry the price of war—
the moods, the darkness,
the fight, the struggle.
We believe in something better—
yet it is the picture within the frame,
the beautiful picture,
that seems two-dimensional.
We cannot enter that picture
from our three-dimensional lives
for we carry a third dimension of darkness.
My heart cries for the scene on the wall

the brook flowing, people smiling.
We want it.
We go to the brook
only to have the day cloud over.
It is their picture—
our frame broke long ago and we can't fix it.

It is the way of war.

We are survivors of war.

The Edge of Faith

I'm so lonely
it hurts.
I've done everything you asked, God.
I'm dizzy with fear—
I see no options.
The pain spins.
The world spins.
Waves of nausea accompany the spinning.

I'm dying
for someone to hold me —
I want to feel love,
I have so much trouble feeling love.
God, I am confused,
but it feels like you're letting me down.
I've laid on your alter
one too many times.
It looks like a beautiful day out there.
I'm so far in here, it's like watching
through an eyeglass.

It doesn't matter—
I can't use any of it
to stop the steady throb.

I feel guilty
I'm doing it wrong.
I'm not learning the lessons—
_____ you God!

You know I need to say it, don't mean it.
Maybe saying it will help.

Sometimes it feels like nothing helps.

I am tormented
and
I am
spent.

November 22, 1963

The sign outside
John J. Pershing
Elementary School says
"Drug Free, Gun Free
School Zone."

On November 22, 1963
Mother takes us from school,
unusual,
to witness the parade.

He is riding in a
Lincoln Continental convertible;
his wife wears
a pink pillbox hat.
They're accompanied
by a man
who will
never be king.

Smack dab in the heart of
Republican North Dallas,
it was bewildering then,
a precursor of
things to come.

We live on the wrong side
of the tracks;
we are Democrats
in a school that is
the immigrants' dream
for their children.

I am a minor troublemaker—
get sent home from school

for chewing gum;
am told by the P.E. coach
that I'll never amount
to anything.
Bring no
guns
or
drugs
to school.

Am disturbed by that
Lord of the Flies
incident in 7th grade.

I hate as
boys carry me,
threaten to
pull down my pants.
I still carry scars
of possible
bone-chilling humiliation.
Girls might see my underwear,
my pubescent penis
in hairless pasture.

I remember—
the librarian,
the art teacher, Miss Lambert,
(I fantasize that she is a "Miss"),
the P.E. coach,
my friends,
John and Harrison;
we search for snakes
in the old country creek
that flows behind a

wealthy neighborhood school.

I remember—
the bright orange hair
of Jack's nephew,
Fred Ruby
as the gentiles
toss pennies
and Fred picks them up
to the taunts of
"*Jew,*" "*Jew.*"

I remember a few hours later—
as we sit in our classroom,
the principal announces
that JFK is dead.
I remember the confusion,
the shattered dream,
the fact that
Mother had taken us
from that
holiest of grails,
education,
to see Mr. President.

But most angrily,
most hauntingly,
I remember
that three or four
children
stand and clap
when they hear
the announcement.

When I look at the signs now,
heavy with loss, I think:
You! You are responsible!

It's your parents'
John Birch Republican
small-minded,
scared-to-death
reactionary
arrogant
legacy
that we live with today.

The signs are signs
born of hatred
and they are
yours.

Photograph of the author, circa 1953, frame © carolyn h. manosevitz,1996.

Who Am I/Who I Am

Self-Portrait

I look in the mirror
and who do I see?
A part of me afraid to look,
another part vain.
So serious,
often so serious.
A complex understanding
and misunderstanding
of the world.
Gentle compassion, love, and sadness
in deep brown eyes
whose penetration
transcends any lifetime.
I see a brow of determination
and delicate hands meant to write
Although I look hard, I know
that I am missing something—
there's something about me
I want to tell you,
but I don't know how

yet.

Faces and Masks

I feel like an actor.
I feel like a fraud.
I go through the motions
as if in a motion picture
with underpowered projector;
the world moves too slowly
as I stumble from one unreality
to the next, trying on
first one cape,
then another,
in a vain attempt
to quench my never-ending thirst
for me.

To the outside world
I accomplish my goals,
but an echo rings hollow
in the cavernous void inside—
the need for more
bouncing within my
cage of ribs,
the exhaustion of being in a play
with curtain raised
for forty years
takes its toll.

Is everyone's desert forty years?

I'm tired of playing a role
in my own life,
of being an actor, a puppet
on strings of my imagination,
moored nowhere,

a lifeline without anchor
drifting aimlessly with
no safe harbor.

The cloak becomes too heavy.
Trying futilely
to make them smile,
my heart cracks under
the weight of the pain.

Cracking is not all bad.

I look at my heart
and see between the cracks.
Light seeps,
then radiates out
in beams of truth.
Afraid at first to let
go of my old heart,
I now watch it crumble;
its case has been a cocoon
and I've been captive
of its illusion of safety.

A wing emerges
and tenuously
I consider flying.
Often I try to shield my
eyes from the light,
turning in fear from the face
of life and truth
Itself.

It's funny—
I have no stage fright as an actor
but I shiver
when I remove the cloak.

I see the Garden of Eden
and am invited in
but I'm afraid to go back home
where everyone can see me
without armour
or shield.
No Greek masks of
tragedy and comedy protect me,
while I turn to
hide my face.

The light blinds me
as the bush continues to
burn within my heart.
I seek the bush
and its eternal flames,
throw the cloak onto the flames
and watch as it is captured
on the thorns of life.
The cloak is strong; it resists.
As I watch it burn, I notice
that the flames
smooth the spikes of the thorns—
an unlikely union of opposites;
integral to each other
in life as well as death;
each a disguise in its own right.

I step from behind the bush
in fresh robe and bare feet.
I stand up straight
on gently cooling grasses.
Although the robe is light
I remove it and walk forward.
For this time it is me
and I am ready to be seen.

My Children Ask

My children ask,
"What can we do on Yom Kippur?"
I really don't know anymore.
I am part of many worlds.
My grandfather sleeps in his shul tonight
so that he can fully observe Yom Kippur.
A couch is sufficient for an 89-year-old man,
close to God.
My father prays at home,
too far to walk to his synagogue.
Is he sad that he can
no longer join a Yom Kippur Minyon?
I go to Kol Nidre for
the first time in years.
We all observe in our own ways.

I don't know, Children, how you should observe.
My grandfather tells, my father suggests.
I abandon and then come back,
searching for God
in the camouflage of religion;
then look back to my father
and grandfather for answers.

The answers are not easy anymore.

Let's begin with the blasphemy of writing.

One simply does not write
on Yom Kippur, but I am writing.
Is this blasphemy or
the perfection of worship?
You must decide for yourselves, Children.
Ancient scales are often difficult to balance—
two parts old, one part new,

fasting on Yom Kippur,
fast food on the Sabbath.

God is very personal for me, Children.
The world has changed,
and it's no longer up to me,
or my father, or grandfather
to dictate your covenant
with your own god.

I'm afraid that in this confusion
of the New World, I haven't given you
a very clear message. I suppose
my father fears the same thing.

I don't know the meaning of the Holocaust,
but I have to believe, Children,
that God wanted something
for us and from us, so God overthrew
hundreds of years of traditions and gave us
a new space on an old slate and the opportunity
to create a direct relationship with God—
not based on the form of your life, the form
of your synagogue, or the form of your worship,
but based on your unbridled imagination and zeal,
and the infinity of your hearts.

It's not about temples, or Rabbis,
or kosher, or even fasting.
It's all about love,
and it's all about your hearts.
I'm still working on my path, Children.
I hope I've given you some
guidance to help with yours.

Tears of a Woman

My wife cries;
I watch from a place far away
as I sit next to her.

Her tears are a curiosity.
Strange, that after all these years
I have so little understanding
of the tears of a woman.

Expression far beyond my reach
this simple act of surrender,
of joy, sadness, anger,
or simply of love
passes from womb to womb,
mother to daughter.

My mother cried;
I couldn't fix it.
A boy, like a man, needs to fix it.
I stood helplessly,
watching my mother's tears.

Did Sarah cry when Abraham
took Isaac to the mountain?
And when they returned,
did her eyes well once more?
What untold mysterious emotions
pulsed in the breast of that woman,
risen in the acts of both
the slaughter
and the redemption,
as all men are slaughterers
and all are redeemers?

My wife cries.
My mother cried.
Sarah cried.
My daughter will cry.
I saw tears in my grandmother's eyes
uncovered in the Shabbas candlelight.

I watch through dry and distant eyes
this enigmatic river of restricted passage.
I seek my own tears
but find instead a dry and barren wadi,
where water occasionally trickles
in the middle of the desert.

Answers Within

I woke up running away
looking out there for answers.

Calculating, analyzing;
building a case,
tearing it down
building a case,
tearing it down,
analysis
paralysis;
gnawing unknowing
of evasive answers.

Slippery and cunning
ego kindles fear
like lightning igniting
dancing forest fires,
an inferno of insanity.
Like cogs of an endless wheel
methodically searching, sorting, spitting
searching, sorting, and
spitting
stream of
idea after
idea.

Obsession!!!

I walk around the lake
looking into the face of
each oncoming traveler.
I am here for a reason!
Someone must have the answer!
Yet my gaze hazingly stares
from stubby face

to bouncing breast
to running shoe
in impossible search.

My world is small—
no hundred-year-old trees
crisp morning
or shimmering lake,

no life
death
or connection,

only searching,
barren searching.

The race is on,
a marathon without end,
searching outside
for answers within.

answers within.

        answers

                    within.

More Like Gandhi

I want to be like Gandhi
sitting cross-legged and so wise.
I want his dedication, his commitment.
Most of all, I want his clarity of vision,
but have no loincloth to cover my warts,
my bruises, and my confusion.

I want the right words to say
but feel tongue-tied and twisted,
embarrassed by my weakness.

Others see my gifts and tell me of them,
but their words ring hollow in my heart.

I want to be more like Gandhi
because Gandhi would've loved me
in spite of my inability
to love myself fully—
the warts, the bruises, and the confusion
evaporating,
invisible,
creations of mortal imagination
seen as love
kissed by the spirit of his eyes,
as the spirit of God passes
through his diminuitive body.

I want to be a seeker
and I want to be a teacher.
I want to let go of the illusion
and live in the truth.
He would've accepted me for who I am.

That was his gift:
he accepted himself.
I want to be more like Gandhi.

The Journey

I stand on the shoulders of those behind me.
I reach for galaxies
unreachable by those who thrust me forward.
Catapulted from the womb of my ancestors
through the looking glass and
looking back, we can
never really see each other again.

I stand for a moment with one foot in each reality—
this moment feels like eons.
Unable to return to the past, I am forced
through uncharted waters
through hurricane and maelstrom
through gales that nearly drown me,
inundated with the waters of change.

Soaked to the core and
weak from the beating,
my body shrinks back,
limp on its journey,
while my soul presses forward
in quiet determination,
a solitary traveler on the eternal journey.

Through windstorm and scorching sun
through crystal clear waters
and tropical paradise
the journey continues,
sweeping me along.
From time to time, the waters dry
and the clouds begin to scatter.
Fear beseeches me to turn back
but I cannot get off.
I've only a one way ticket,
destination stamped: "LIFE."

Flipping Channels

My dog is eating grass this morning.
Perhaps she has decided to become a vegetarian
or maybe to imitate a dim-witted ruminant or herbivore.
She has a great imagination
for a dog.

Why should we be any different?
We spend most of our lives imitating others.

I object to television.

A nice couple with three small collie-looking dogs
drops by for a visit.
Their dogs hover close
while Lucy runs round
in huge patterns
of her own mind
as if on a runway
reaching maximum thrust
for outer space.
I am glad that she enjoys her freedom.

It's funny:
usually I walk her
taking her wherever I want to go.
It gets mundane.

The best trips
are when I sit still
and she takes my imagination
all over her runway.

It's so hard to be still.
It's also the gift of the artist, or yogi,
seeing the motion picture

one frame at a time.
We meditate with eyes wide open,
painting a still life
while the daily world whirrs by
to its own rhythm, its chaos.

My friend asks why we can't spend
all of our time on the mountain.
Ask Moses.
It's too bright up there.
Most of us are not ready for eternal brightness.
Most of us shy away.
Moses had work to do
so God sent him back.
Most of us wish that God
would stop sending us back.
Perhaps that is the lesson—
we look to the mountain
and back at our own lives, confused.
It's like watching television.

Absolutely nothing that we see on television is true.
Absolutely everything that we see on television is true.

God sends us back to pay attention.
He subtly reminds us that we
are just as ready for the mountain
as we are for our own lives.
We could live there in confusion
just as easily.

I fancy myself a poet, a writer.
My mountain is wherever
I sit still and write.
I do it about one hair's breadth of my time.
The rest of the time I'm on television.

Perhaps I'm on television all of the time,
flipping channels in a vain attempt
to find the right picture.

I like to blame the television.

The television is my mind.

A family, grandparents, parents,
a small child walk by
speaking a language I do not recognize.
Why did they interrupt this program?
I want to control each station.
Perhaps our channels got crossed.
They speak Portuguese
or Italian
or Babel.
They are no different
from everyone I encounter—
we rarely stop to understand each other.

My channel selector tells me
it's time to leave,
to change channels.
My channel selector is broken;
it refuses to stay focused on one channel.

It's a glorious day!
I give up.
I think I'll go home.
I can't!
I haven't had enough.
Today the mountain is sweet;
I quench my thirst from its many nectars.

Suddenly, I am afraid.
I feel it subtly in my chest, my heart.
IT'S O.K.! I've learned
to sometimes allow the fear
channel to run its course.
It has a mind of its own.
If left to its own devices, it usually
runs its course quickly.

I want to leave.
I am afraid to leave.
It laughs at me.
Ha ha ha ha ha ha ha ha!

Lucy comes,
tries to muzzle me
with her lake-stained face.
It helps, though I am not
interested in her muddy kiss.

I am afraid of the aloneness, the terror.
It is just one of my channels.
The aloneness channel is
black and white, mostly black.
Although it is short-lived,
it comes in powerful pulses,
daily waves of flu infecting my body.
I have antibodies.
I will recover.

Two butterflies change the channel. . . .

Up the Mountain With Misplaced Paddle

I don't even know how I got up here.
How am I supposed to get down?
Rocks are sliding.
The Earth is sliding.
I am sliding.
Cacti are everywhere.
Their thorns could impale me.
I don't know how to get down!
How did I get up here?
My friends are below.
The small voice in my stomach
cries out for help.
Of course they don't hear it.
Help me down!
I don't know how to get down!
I'm ready to go.
The blood throbs in my forehead.
I don't know which way to go!!!

Suddenly, I just climb down.

Big Bend National Park • Pine Canyon • October 19, 1995

Who I Was

What you remember
is who I
was.

I may not even be
that person anymore.

Even though
you saw me
yesterday,
don't try to
pin that
on me

because
that's not
who I
am. It's
who I
was.

"faces and masks I," 30" x 20," mixed media, © carolyn h. manosevitz, 1995.

Everything Changes

Enchanted Oak

One fine
gnarled oak—
your legs are twisted
yet your head stands high and
your arms dance in the wind.

Sole oak on the mountaintop
all of life's forces sought to
blow you away,
yet you made it.

You are my teacher
I am reverent in your presence.

Enchanted Rock • May 18, 1995

Different Place

I'm sitting in a different place
at Laguna Gloria.
I don't like it.
It's too secluded.
Although the breezes are strong,
it's feeling kind of claustraphobic in here.

Lucy sloshes around in
foul-smelling mud.
She loves this spot
on the point.
I worry about her
encountering a water moccasin.
She thinks she smells great.

The mud is like my thinking.
A friend says his mind
is a dangerous neighborhood—
he tries not to go there too often.

Lucy sloshes mud flecks on
my new jacket,
the one with *Timberland*
written on the sleeve.
I am so proud.

Lucy yelps,
then returns.
Water moccasin?

I slosh through the mud
of my mind,
filled to the eyes
with thick, molasses-like thoughts.
Occasionally, a thought gurgles

up to the top, and
pops!
into the light,
but the gravity of the bog
slurps it back inward,
slurring throat-based chortles
of gasping suffocation
into the mysterious stillness.
I am committed
to escaping the bog.
What an arduous task!

Why, on my way to Ithaca,
did I drop into the Inferno?

Moses Wuz Lonely

Moses takes a walk one morning
and looks down into the land of Canaan.
"Where am I, O' Lord?," he asks.
"I've been wandering round this
desert for forty years,
searching for answers.
The desert is not that big.
And now I think I have the answer,
O' Lord, Canaan.
But once again, is it really the answer?
Won't you please tell me the answer?" he cries.

"You were never in the desert," replies the Lord.
"It's only the way you looked at it."

No Place to Write

No time to write today.
I'm spending way too much time
searching for a writing spot,
climbing up slippery mountains,
ducking under thorny brush.
My mother would be frightened—
she would think I am in danger

of falling. I've been falling
my whole life without ever letting go.

I forget the danger.
I'm just rooting around,
looking for a place to write.

Instead, I find an annoying mosquito,
see the sun shimmering white light
around glorious mountaintops,
watch pine trees in shadows
of boulders which will fall soon—
in the next ten or twenty thousand years.

The pines are beautiful,
and comfortable in their peace—
Do I dare warn them of the boulders?

Mother would.

It would be important for her
to warn them of the danger.

I am surrounded by desert flowers—
tiny yellow six-part blossoms,
pink teacups, purple buds.
There are cacti right below me.

Should I be careful not to
slip and fall into them
or write of their subtle victories?

I am with friends;
they seem ready to leave.
Should I hurry? It took
so long to find this spot.
There are better spots
I know there are better spots.
This spot is hard.
There is no soft space
to lean back.
My buttocks ache from the
hard pillow of rock.
There's no way I can write here.

Perhaps where Bruce is.
That looks like a better spot.
Or Mark, he climbed higher;
it must be better.
Or Mel, who stopped before
and again now.
He found two places to write!

I look up at the desert waterfall
and down to the dry pool below,
filled with autumn leaves.
I see mountains, hazy in their distance
and a rock wall of a
million facets on my right.
I see an ice cool, moistureless
pale blue sky clear to heaven
and the verdant songs of
Pine Canyon stretching below.

I see tall grasses,
infinite rocks from shards
to continents.
I see a canopy of trees
and left-handed shadows.
I hear the voices of fall
and the voices of friends.
I see sights so stupendous
that I can't begin to describe them.

I see all this,
but I've still found
no place to write.

Big Bend National Park • Pine Canyon • October 19, 1995

Three's a Crowd

It's interesting—
I came here with friends,
yet I long to be alone.
Something doesn't feel
quite complete yet.

The night is black radiance
and I steal some time for myself.
I travel with soulmates,
but thirst for companions
of another sort.

The Pleiades, for instance.
I need to look at them and wonder,
to feel insignificant, yet connected.
The Chisos surround me.
I need to feel cradled
in their mountainous hands.
I crave being alone in my tent at night,
snug within my four walls of nylon—
feeling more secure in nylon
than ever in stone and mortar.

The voices of strangers
strangely fill me in a way
impossible for the voices of friends.

It's a sense of connection I get
from throwing off all the trappings
that are supposed to secure me
and putting on my robe of personal wonders.

I see a shooting star
and am not surprised.
When I am alone here

and stop,
I expect God to share his many favors
and am never disappointed.
I come here to expand my world,
which I can't do by talking.

It's a solitary job—
not lonely, just solitary.

Sometimes three's a crowd when looking for God.

Big Bend National Park • Chisos Mountain Basin• October 20, 1995
In the Starlit Sky with Flashlight

Windmill at Glen Springs

At twilight, I sit quietly waiting
for evening's magic at Glen Springs.
Before we lived in ghettos, we were
people of the earth. Our noble ancestry is
that of capable men, men skilled
in hunting
 loving
 living
 crying
 and dying
We were not afraid.

The ancient windmill spins
round and round,
darting in one direction, then the next,
like men spinning and darting.

The rugged Chisos lie off to my right,
a black-cragged monolith, as the sun lights
a face I can no longer see, while to my left
the impossibly brilliant pink-white face
of the Sierra del Carmens is kissed goodnight
by evening's sun.

Having shut off the deafening din
of my life's everyday desert, I deeply breathe
the subtle sounds of life—
the winds rustling in the cottonwoods. . . birdtalk. . .
the gentle buzz of my personal kamikaze fly. . .
the satisfied breath flowing out from my body. . . .

Earlier today, I rushed from nowhere to nowhere.
Everywhere becomes nowhere when I rush.
As I stop the rushing shifts—

I see fresh rustling leaves dance in rushing winds.
I feel a gently rushing breeze cool my sun-baked face.
I see the fly busily rush to some place unknown.
It is life's paradox.

Einstein was right—
the faster we move, the more of a blur it becomes.
Einstein was a capable man.
We are all Einstein's brothers.

Big Bend National Park• Dugout Wells • April 7, 1995

God Winked

God winked
and for once I saw it,
as I walked along the trail
out from the chilly morning basin
along the sunkissed ridge.

God winked.
Normally I wouldn't have noticed
but something caught my eye.

God winked.
I looked into the meadow
and saw the two deer—
first the doe then the young buck.
Each of us was immediately aware
and at peace in the other's presence,
for they accepted me not as intruder
but as fellow wanderer.
They wander the meadow.
I wander the trail.

God winked.
They grazed nearby.
How did they know they were
safe in my spirit?

Big Bend National Park• Laguna Meadows • South Rim Trail • October 1994

The Banks of Laguna Gloria

The leaves have
started to fall
on the banks of Laguna Gloria.

Chinese tallows
drip blood-red
and fire-yellow feathers.

My dog is happy.
Her hind leg quivers
as she runs large
circles from lake to sky
and back again.

Monolithic sculptures surround me.
Ferns grow out of the shoulder of one
while my dog sniffs curiously
at the base of another.

Birds scream at each other
across the clearing.
It is still warm. Tallows molt
while it is still warm here.

My dog disappears for a moment
leaving me at peace,
then returns from yet another
jaunt to her Mars, or Venus.

A distant phone rings—
it is no trouble;
I know it is not mine.

A dove flies across the clearing.
Usually they are in
pairs. I pause for a moment,
then realize we are a pair.

My dog returns from another
foray. Tiring now, she
can't help herself, heads
for the water once more.
Now she runs to me full speed
to let me know how happy she is.
Thank God, she shook
the water off elsewhere.

A yellow butterfly flies by. I open
my mouth to see if it will fly in.
I feel like I could stay here forever.

I notice that the grass is covered with dew.
I'd never have seen that
if I'd gone to work today.

Spirits of the Wind

We are people of the desert;
I am at home here.
The ancient connection
to lives long past
who wandered from Egypt,
spirits swirl in the wind;
my ancestors cool the sweat that
soaks my back
as I climb to meet them.

Perched on a ledge
high above the desert floor,
I see cactus and pine in
apparent contradiction.
It is God's trick,
God's way of illustrating
that all is one.

My memories of that desert
I wandered from Egypt
are not bad. There was
something comforting
in my freedom then, as it
is comforting now to feel the cool
breeze in the warm midmorning sun.

We wander in places
like this through many lifetimes.
Our ancient recall reminds us
we have all been Moses
seeking God on the mountain,
for we are all Moses, and
God speaks to each of us.

My ancestors sweep around me,
dancing in the wind . . .

Raven

A lone raven sits
atop a crag, on a
pillar of rock jutting what
seems like a thousand feet
from the desert floor below.

Is that you, God?
Dozing in the partial shade
of a dwarf oak, I
hear you call.

Nice sense of humor, God.
A year ago, *Spirits of the Wind,*
today, a raven.

I watch you spread your wings
to warm in the sun's glow.
It's only a year since
you started telling me stories.
Now you make a strange sound—
aarumpf
aarumpf
aarumpf
aarumpf
from deep within your throat.
What does it mean, God?

Your mate gently soars overhead,
calls out another message
I am unable to decipher.
What's the message today, God?

And all of a sudden, you are gone.

Big Bend National Park• Lost Mine Trail • October 20, 1995

Blurred Lines

Sitting at graduation, watching
my daughter's choir float
through *America the Beautiful*,
squinting to see my daughter,
I remember my grandmother.

I remember holding my daughter,
pink skin still of the sea
in front of my grandmother
as she nears her death.

Grandmother, can you see her?, I plead.
She tells me she can't see. Her blindness,
now advanced, provides cloudy
evening light, fuzzy edged shapes,
sporadic night cave darkness.

The salutatorian jokes about
clothing under graduation gowns.

But Grandmother, can't you see her,
just a little? I beg, twist, and turn her
in every conceivable direction.

Introduced by the retiring principal,
the valedictorian takes the stage.

Look Grandmother, it's your
great-granddaughter. Isn't she
beautiful? Isn't this
wonderful? Don't you
love her?

The valedictorian speaks
rapidly of feelings. I
drift off, dream of myself
standing by Grandmother's
skirt. Waist high, I look
up for the wonders she
shares from the kitchen stove.

The valedictorian tells how her father
died when she was in the first grade.

But Grandmother, can't you
see her just a little?
Perhaps remembering the warm
stovetop, Grandmother looks up,
says, *Yes, I can see her,*
just a little. I want to believe her.

I still have the picture, black and white,
of her hollow stare as she holds my daughter.

The clear-eyed graduates
parade across the stage.

You lie in a coma, Grandmother,
for five long months; Grandfather
tries futilely to save you. What do you see
as you drift peacefully into dark,
as you float down, down, down?

I imagine you looking back
through your life, dozing in,
drifting out. . .the war. . .
escape to America. . .success. . .
your sons' deaths. . .your life. . .
the Shabbas Candlelight. . . .

Grandmother, I pretend
you join me as I
tightly hold your skirt
and you stir the
soup of memory
now cool on top of
the idle kitchen stove.

Grandmother

Grandmother—I'm here
with you in the steady candlelight.
Your love bathes me often.
I know that you are with me, smiling.

Where are you spending Yom Kippur,
Grandmother? Are you
dancing with Isaac and Ben?
Are the Holocaust Klezmorim
playing a hora for 6 million spirits?
It must be crowded with joy,
O' Grandmother.

Why is our connection so strong?
Why am I so fortunate to
find you everywhere?
You have seen my pain and you
have always been there, smiling
O' Grandmother.

You have joined the spirits of eons
and you jump out from them
alone in the candlelight.
What is it about candlelight
that calls us together?
Being with you calls forth
the hum of a Yiddishe tune;
though I have trouble remembering
such a tune in my head,
the cello resonates in my heart
with a tune I can never forget.

Oif in pripiczyk brent a fire-u
The flame burns on the stovetop
unt in shteib is heis.

as it warms the room.
Dort sitzt e Rebele
There the teacher sits
mit kleine kinderlech
with small children,
lernen aleph-beis.
learning their a-b-c's.

I hear songs of
loved ones no longer present
in a limited sense.

Dort sitzt e Rebele
mit kleine kinderlech,
lernen aleph-beis.

For Helen Beck

She looked into my eyes
and said, almost pleaded,
*Think big. And go
for your dreams.*

She was no ordinary person
this tiny
ray
of
light,
survivor of
Auschwitz.

She told of the horrors,
praised Shindler,
who had saved *her*
among 299 other women,
told how she
had been brutally shaved
by *SS men*,
put into a gas chamber where she
looked into the shower head, pressed
naked flesh to naked flesh, and
waited for the cyanide. She told how
suddenly, by some miracle,
water, o' glorious water,
came gushing through the jets.

She told how, after the war,
she found her baby sister
dirty and shivering,
under a railway station bench.

With glowing eyes
she told of her sons,
her grandchildren.

So much to say,
so little time.
So much to say,
so little time.

She told me all
of this and then
so simply, so indomitably,
she encouraged *me*
to go for my dreams.

The big ones.

The Dancer

I am the dancer, hopping lightly
from toe to toe. I dance the spirit
of God's song—if you peek, you will
see the silhouette of my image, dancing
along the top rail of your fence.

I dance a mystical dance
thousands of years old.
Look closely and you'll recognize me—
you were there when I danced this
dance before. You danced it yourself once,
don't you remember?

I saw you gliding effortlessly to the melodies
of the wind, the crickets, and the shooting stars.
You danced in a silent symphony of moonlight—
don't you remember?

You didn't know I saw, and you honestly
feign no recollection of your early
heart's song. You believe your feet are
stuck to the ground, but I saw you and
I know that you can dance.

Please join me. We'll dance together,
each of us dancing our solitary dance of light.
Together we will bathe the earth
with the glow of our dance. Just for
that fleeting moment, the fireflies will light
in unison as our spirits gently intertwine,
twirling without touching, while we
momentarily disappear into the oneness of God.

Big Bend National Park• Chisos Mountain Basin• October, 1994

94

Everything Changes

Taking it in;
a journey is an unwinding.
I watch the lone American flag
hang limply in the gentle bath
of midmorning sun, imagining
soldiers and Indians.
Military marches blaring
over military loudspeakers
fade, as suddenly I notice the
tall winter grasses, dried
and dancing, as they rustle
timelessly golden to the songs
of birds of whose faces I am
ignorant but whose melodies I love.

The grasses were here
before the cavalry, yes,
before even the natives.
Perhaps a soldier
sitting on this very rock
noticed the grasses for a moment
as he paused in his life,
unwinding from daily work
to experience God's journey.

My pen rises to greet me,
to rejoice in this moment.
I notice the wind on my cheek
as if touched by angel's wings.

The buildings round me crumble,
relics of human imagination,
our drive to control the world.
Our powerful dreams frequently
crumble as the grasses
continue to blow.

I look up and notice the flag
standing stiffly in the
heightening breeze.

Everything changes.

Ft. Davis • Davis Mountains • April 3, 1995.

Epilogue

Holocaust:

I've already given you half a life.
You want the rest.

You are a jealous, evil mistress—
we dance together
in an empty dark space
of hollow black skeletons.

You steal
my spirit
my joy
my strength
my serenity.

You rob me of my consciousness
and fill me with
anger
greed
and fear.

I dance with a devil,
sunken eyes filled with
deep-set gold-glowing
embers of evil.

You dance circles on
the graves of spirits
and, stupefied, I dance along,
an unconscious accomplice.

Constantly, unerringly,
the anxiety creeps into my mind,
goose bumps rise on my shoulders,

control churns me forward
plodding elliptically
on a dark stage.

Holocaust:
You have tormented my family
and my family's family.
You birth corpses
surrounded by flesh,
rotting on the inside.

You are an evil experiment
of lasting consequence.

I've given you half a life.
You'll have to fight me for the rest.

Either God is everything
or
God is nothing.

About the Author

Stan Biderman (benhocohanim) was born in Dallas, Texas in 1951. After WWII, the fragments of his family which survived the war migrated to north Texas. His first language was Yiddish, spoken with a Texas accent.

Biderman earned B.B.A. and J.D. degrees from the University of Texas. After practicing law for fifteen years, he now divides his time between a business career and writing. He lives in Austin with his wife, Linda, and almost-grown children, Andrea and Zach.

His collaborations with visual artist Carolyn Manosevitz have resulted in a highly regarded touring exhibit exploring the common experiences of second generation Holocaust survivors. Inquiries regarding programs, art exhibits, readings and workshops can be sent to Stan Biderman, P.O. Box 50125, Austin, TX 78763-0125.

About the Artist

Carolyn H. Manosevitz was born and raised in Winnipeg, Canada. She received a B.A. cum laude from the University of Minnesota and an MFA from the University of Texas. She has been involved in the arts for over 20 years as a visual artist/educator and creativity consultant.

Manosevitz has exhibited widely both in the United States and Canada. Her work is part of private and corporate collections in the U.S., Canada and Israel. Paintings from this series are now part of permanent collections at the Ghetto Fighter's Museum and Yad Vashem in Israel.

Manosevitz began a series of collaborations with Stan Biderman in 1995. The resulting work has been presented in exhibits, readings and lectures in Texas, Arkansas, Colorado, California, Ohio, New York and will be part of an exhibit at the B'nai B'rith Klutznick National Jewish Museum in Washington, D. C. in 1998 to commemorate the 60th anniversary of Krystallnacht.